You Are Unstoppable.

Personal & Small Group Study Guide

Overcome Setbacks. Experience Breakthroughs (2nd Edition)

Dr. Mike Prah

Published by Mpaebo Media a division of Mike Prah, LLC, Severn, MD. www.mikeprah.com

U. S. Library of Congress Cataloging-in-Publication Data

Prah, Mike, Author

You are unstoppable. personal & small group study guide : Overcome setbacks. experience breakthroughs (2nd edition) / Mike Prah.

Second Edition, 2026.

Severn, Maryland : Mpaebo Media, 2026 | Includes Scripture references, discussion questions, personal reflection guides, and daily believer declarations.

pages cm

ISBN 979-8-9906475-2-7 (paperback)

ISBN 978-1-969340-17-8 (ebook)

Subjects: LCSH: Christian life—Study and teaching | Christian life—Biblical teaching | Spiritual formation—Christianity | Discipleship—Christianity | Bible—Study and teaching.

Classification: BV4501.3.P73 2026 | DDC 248.4—dc23

LCCN: 1-15154463481

Printed in the United States of America

Special Bulk Discounts and Custom Editions:

Most books authored by Mike Prah are available at special discounted rates for bulk purchases by churches, organizations, businesses, and individuals. Customized editions or book excerpts can also be created to meet the specific needs of your ministry, event, or audience. For more information or to inquire about a special order, please contact: info@mikeprah.com. Available through major U.S. and international online book retailers. Signed copies are also available from the author.

Direct purchases are available at http://mikeprah.com/bookstore

WELCOME LETTER

Dear Friend,

Welcome to *You Are Unstoppable. Personal & Small Group Study Guide*. I'm truly honored that you've chosen to take this journey.

Whether you're working through this guide on your own or with a group, my prayer is simple: that you experience real transformation. Life has a way of presenting challenges—setbacks, fears, habits, disappointments, and wounds that can quietly hold us back. At times, it may feel like you're stuck or not living up to your full potential. But I want you to know something clearly—**God has more for your life.**

This study guide was created to help you move forward with clarity, confidence, and faith. Each session is designed to be practical, biblical, and engaging—helping you not only understand God's truth but apply it to your daily life. As you walk through these sessions, I encourage you to be open, honest, and intentional. Growth happens when we are willing to reflect, learn, and take action.

If you're in a group, lean into the discussions. There is power in shared experiences, encouragement, and accountability. If you're studying on your own, take your time—pause, pray, and allow God to speak to you personally.

A Prayer for You

Heavenly Father, I lift up every person reading this guide. You know their story, their struggles, and their desires. I ask that You would strengthen them, guide them, and remind them of Your purpose for their lives. Where there is fear, bring courage. Where there is confusion, bring clarity. Where there is pain, bring healing.

Lord, let this journey be a turning point. Help them grow in faith, walk in truth, and experience the fullness of the life You have prepared for them. In Jesus' name, Amen.

No matter where you are right now—whether you feel strong or struggling—this is your opportunity to take the next step forward.

Your past does not define you. Your challenges do not disqualify you.With God's help, you can overcome—and you are unstoppable.

Grace and peace,

Mike Prah

CONTENTS

Introduction

Life is filled with opportunities—but it is also filled with obstacles. At some point, we all encounter challenges that test our faith, stretch our character, and threaten to limit our potential. These challenges may come in the form of setbacks, fear, unhealthy habits, leadership pressures, personal weaknesses, or deep emotional wounds. The question is not whether we will face these obstacles—but how we will respond to them.

You Are Unstoppable. Personal & Small Group Study Guide is designed to help you respond with faith, wisdom, and strength. This guide is built on biblical principles that empower you to overcome what holds you back and step into the life God has called you to live. Each session addresses a key area of growth, providing practical insight and spiritual direction for real-life transformation.

Throughout this study, you will explore how to:

- Live an overflowing life rooted in God's provision

- Turn setbacks into stepping stones for success

- Clarify your vision and pursue your God-given purpose

- Overcome fear and internal struggles

- Break free from destructive habits and strongholds

- Develop character-driven leadership

- Live a life of significance and lasting impact

- Grow stronger through weakness

- Recover from life's hurts and move forward with hope

Each session is structured to help you engage both personally and relationally. You'll find icebreakers, reflection questions, Scripture-based discussions, practical applications, and prayer prompts designed to guide you step by step.

This study can be used in two ways:

Personal Study

Take time to reflect, journal, and pray through each session. Move at a pace that allows the truths to take root in your heart and life.

Small Group Study

Engage in meaningful discussion with others. Share insights, encourage one another, and grow together in accountability and faith.

A Final Word

Transformation does not happen overnight—but it does happen when you commit to growth. As you walk through this study, remember that God is not only interested in what you achieve, but in who you are becoming.

He is working in you, strengthening you, shaping you, and preparing you for more.

An Invitation

If you are reading this and realize that you've been trying to do life on your own, I want to gently remind you—you were never meant to walk this journey alone. The strength, purpose, and transformation described in this guide begin with a relationship with Jesus Christ.

He is not only the Savior who forgives, but the Lord who leads, strengthens, and restores.

If you would like to begin that relationship today, you can simply pray:

A Simple Prayer

Lord Jesus, I come to You just as I am. I acknowledge that I need You. Thank You for loving me and giving Your life for me. Forgive me of my sins and come into my life.

Be my Savior and my Lord. Guide my steps, strengthen my faith, and help me become the person You created me to be.

From this day forward, I choose to follow You. In Jesus' name, Amen.

If you prayed that prayer sincerely, you've taken the most important step of your life. Continue seeking God through His Word, prayer, and connection with other believers.

With God's power at work in you, your best days are still ahead. You are unstoppable.

How to Use This Study Guide

This study guide is designed to help you grow spiritually, think biblically, and live intentionally. Whether you are using it on your own or with a group, each session is structured to move you from understanding to transformation.

OVERVIEW

This guide contains 10 sessions, each focused on a key area of personal and spiritual growth. Every session follows a consistent format to help you engage fully:

- **Session Aim** — What you will learn and experience

- **Ice Breaker** — A simple question to build connection

- **Opening Prayer** — Invite God into your time

- **Introduction** — A brief overview of the topic

- **Bible Discussion**

    - *Personalizing the Message* — Reflect on your life

    - *Digging Deeper* — Explore Scripture and key truths

- **Personal Application & Reflection** — Apply what you've

learned

- **Closing Wisdom Keys** — Key truths to remember

- **Prayer** — Commit your growth to God

FOR PERSONAL STUDY

If you are using this guide on your own:

- Set aside consistent time each week

- Read slowly and thoughtfully—don't rush

- Take time to reflect, journal, and pray

- Be honest with yourself—growth requires honesty

- Focus on application, not just information

Tip: Keep a notebook or journal to track what God is teaching you.

FOR SMALL GROUP STUDY

If you are using this guide in a group setting:

- Begin each session with the Ice Breaker to build connection

- Create a safe, judgment-free environment

- Encourage everyone to participate, but never force sharing

- Stay focused on the discussion, but allow the Holy Spirit to lead

- Respect time, but prioritize meaningful conversation

Leader Tip: Your role is to facilitate, not dominate. Guide the discussion, ask questions, and allow others to share.

MAXIMIZING YOUR EXPERIENCE

To get the most out of this study:

- Come with an open heart and teachable spirit

- Be willing to change and grow

- Apply at least one principle each week

- Stay consistent—even when it feels challenging

- Invite God into every step of the process

A FINAL ENCOURAGEMENT

This is more than a study—it's a journey.

Some sessions may challenge you. Others may encourage or stretch you. At times, you may feel convicted, inspired, or even uncomfortable. That's part of growth.

Don't quit. Don't rush. Don't just read—engage.

God is working in you, even when you don't immediately see it.

As you commit to this process, trust that God will strengthen you, guide you, and help you become the person He created you to be.

You are not stuck. You are not finished.With God, you are moving forward—because you are unstoppable.

HELPFUL TIPS FOR SMALL GROUP HOSTS

Congratulations! By stepping into the role of a small group leader, you are partnering with Jesus in His work as the Good Shepherd. What a privilege and calling! Whether you are leading for a single session or an entire series, remember—you are not alone. God has chosen you, equipped you, and promises, *"He will never leave you nor forsake you"* (Hebrews 13:5, NIV). As you serve His people, you will be blessed along the way.

1. Be Authentic and Welcoming

Be yourself—God intends to use your unique personality and gifts. Greet each person warmly as they arrive. A genuine smile and kind welcome can set the tone for the entire gathering. Remember, showing up may have taken courage for some. Create an environment where people feel seen, valued, and safe. Don't feel pressure to have all the answers. If you're unsure, simply say so. If you make a mistake, own it graciously. Authenticity builds trust and fosters meaningful connection.

2. Prepare with Purpose

Take time before each meeting to review the discussion material. Reflect on the questions and consider your own responses. Most sessions include more content than can be covered in one meeting—prayerfully select the questions that best serve your group's needs. Preparation allows you to lead with confidence and clarity.

3. Facilitate, Don't Dominate

Small groups thrive on conversation, not lectures. Ask questions and allow space for responses. Silence is not your enemy—it often means people are thinking. Resist the urge to fill every pause or teach after each answer.

Affirm contributions with simple encouragement like, *"Thank you for sharing,"* or *"That's a great insight."* Then invite others in: *"Would anyone else like to add?"* Create space for every voice.

4. Guide the Flow with Grace

Invite volunteers to read Scripture or discussion prompts rather than calling on individuals directly. This helps introverts and newer participants feel safe.

If one person tends to dominate, gently redirect the conversation: *"Let's hear from someone who hasn't shared yet."*

Your goal is to cultivate balanced participation where everyone feels included.

Never pressure anyone to share deeply personal details. A safe group allows people to participate at their own pace.

5. Cover Your Group in Prayer

Prayer is the foundation of every effective group. Begin by praying for your members by name. Ask God to guide your time and speak to each heart.

When needs arise during the meeting, pause and pray together. Stay sensitive to the leading of the Holy Spirit. Prayer transforms the atmosphere and deepens spiritual connection.

6. Share the Leadership

You don't have to carry the responsibility alone. Consider inviting a co-leader or rotating facilitation roles. Jesus sent His disciples out in pairs (Luke 10:1), modeling shared ministry.

This not only lightens your load but also strengthens the group by developing others.

7. Honor Time and Commitment

Respect the schedules of your group members. Start and end on time whenever possible. Clear expectations build trust and encourage consistency.

8. Cultivate Joy and Connection

Don't be overly rigid—leave room for genuine connection, laughter, encouragement, and Spirit-led moments. Scripture reminds us, *"A cheerful heart is good medicine"* (Proverbs 17:22, NIV).

A Shepherd's Heart: Prepare Spiritually

Before leading your first session, take time to prayerfully reflect on these Scriptures. Ask God to shape your heart as a shepherd who leads with compassion, humility, and love:

- Matthew 9:36–38

- John 10:14–15

- 1 Peter 5:2–4

- Philippians 2:1–5

- Hebrews 10:23–25

- 1 Thessalonians 2:7–8, 11–12

Let these passages anchor your leadership in Christ's example. As you lead, remember: you are not just guiding a discussion—you are shepherding people God deeply loves.

CHAPTER 1 STUDY GUIDE — LIVING THE OVERFLOWING LIFE

A. SESSION AIM

To help participants shift from a scarcity mindset to a surplus mindset by understanding God's desire for them to live an overflowing life. This session will guide participants to embrace four daily habits that cultivate spiritual abundance, peace, and purpose.

B. ICE BREAKER

If you had a completely free day with no responsibilities, how would you spend it—and why?

Leader Note: Keep responses light and enjoyable. This helps participants relax and begin thinking about what brings them joy and fulfillment.

C. OPEN YOUR SESSION WITH PRAYER

Ask someone to lead in a prayer in their own words, or use the prayer below:

Heavenly Father, we thank You for bringing us together today. Open our hearts and minds to receive Your truth. Help us to see ourselves the way You see us and to embrace the life You've called us to live. Let this time be transformational as we grow in our understanding of You and Your purpose for our lives. In Jesus' name, Amen.

D. INTRODUCTION (CHAPTER 1 SUMMARY)

We live in a culture driven by comparison, pressure, and the fear of missing out. This mindset leaves many people overwhelmed, anxious, and constantly striving for more. Yet God offers a different way to live—an overflowing life. This life is not defined by external success, but by a deep trust in God's provision and goodness. Scripture reveals two contrasting approaches: a scarcity mindset that leads to stress and insecurity, and a surplus mindset that produces peace, contentment, and confidence. Through Psalm 23 and the teachings of Jesus, we see that God desires to fill our lives beyond capacity. This session will explore how to move from overwhelm to overflow by embracing four daily habits rooted in a relationship with God.

E. BIBLE DISCUSSION

SECTION 1: PERSONALIZING THE MESSAGE

1. When do you most feel overwhelmed or "not enough"?

2. In what areas of your life do you feel pressure to keep up with others?

3. Do you tend to think in terms of "not enough" or "more than enough"? Why?

4. What do you believe an "overflowing life" really looks like?

SECTION 2: SCRIPTURE DISCOVERY

KEY POINT 1: Shift from a Scarcity Mindset to a Surplus Mindset

Scriptures: 2 Kings 4:42–44; Philippians 4:19

Scripture Insights: A scarcity mindset focuses on lack and limitation, leading to anxiety and insecurity. A surplus mindset trusts in God's unlimited provision and produces peace and confidence. The overflowing life begins with changing how you think about God and His resources.

Discussion Questions:

1. Read 2 Kings 4:42–44. What is the difference between the servant's response and Elisha's response?

2. How does a scarcity mindset show up in everyday life?

3. Read Philippians 4:19. What does this verse teach about God's provision?

4. How does believing God is your source change your outlook on life?

5. What is one area where you need to shift from scarcity to surplus thinking?

KEY POINT 2: Stay Connected to Jesus Daily

Scriptures: John 15:4–5, 7–11

Scripture Insights: The overflowing life flows from connection, not striving. Just as a branch must remain connected to the vine to bear fruit, we must stay connected to Jesus to experience spiritual strength, joy, and productivity.

Discussion Questions:

1. Read John 15:5. Why does Jesus say we can do nothing without Him?

2. What happens when we try to live life disconnected from God?

3. What are practical ways to stay connected to Jesus daily?

4. How does spending time with God impact your mindset and emotions?

5. What is one change you can make to strengthen your daily connection with God?

KEY POINT 3: Choose Gratitude Over Complaining

Scriptures: Philippians 2:14; Colossians 2:7

Scripture Insights: Complaining drains your energy and perspective, while gratitude fuels joy, peace, and resilience. A grateful heart is essential to living an overflowing life.

Discussion Questions:

1. Read Philippians 2:14. Why does God command us to avoid complaining?

2. How does complaining affect your mindset and relationships?

3. Read Colossians 2:7. What does it mean to "overflow with thanksgiving"?

4. What are some practical ways to develop a habit of gratitude?

5. How can gratitude shift your outlook during difficult seasons?

KEY POINT 4: Choose Contentment Over Comparison

Scriptures: Proverbs 14:30; 1 Timothy 6:6

Scripture Insights: Comparison leads to dissatisfaction and insecurity, while contentment produces peace and stability. True contentment comes from trusting God and valuing what He has already given you.

Discussion Questions:

1. Read Proverbs 14:30. How does comparison affect your emotional health?

2. Why is comparison so common in today's culture?

3. Read 1 Timothy 6:6. What does "godliness with contentment" mean?

4. How can you practice contentment in a comparison-driven world?

5. What is one area where you need to stop comparing yourself to others?

KEY POINT 5: Choose Generosity Over Selfishness

Scriptures: 2 Corinthians 9:6–8; Luke 6:38

Scripture Insights: Generosity reflects trust in God's provision. When you give freely, God blesses you abundantly. The overflowing life is not just about receiving—it is about giving.

Discussion Questions:

1. Read 2 Corinthians 9:6–8. What principle does this passage teach about giving?

2. Why do people struggle with generosity?

3. How does generosity reflect faith in God?

4. Read Luke 6:38. What promise does Jesus give about giving?

5. What is one practical way you can be more generous this week?

F. SECTION 3: PERSONAL APPLICATION & REFLECTION

1. Which mindset—scarcity or surplus—do you most identify with right now?

2. Which of the four habits do you need to strengthen the most?

3. What is one daily practice you will commit to this week?

4. How can you begin living more intentionally from a place of overflow?

G. CLOSING WISDOM TAKE-AWAYS

1. The overflowing life begins when you trust God as your source, not your circumstances.

2. Connection to Christ produces the overflow—disconnection

leads to depletion.

3. Gratitude, contentment, and generosity are the daily pathways to a life that overflows.

H. PRAYER

I. PRAYER POINTS

1. Ask God to help you embrace a surplus mindset

2. Pray for strength to stay connected to Jesus daily

3. Present your personal needs—asking God for provision, peace, and direction

4. Ask the Holy Spirit to cultivate gratitude, contentment, and generosity in your life

II. CLOSING PRAYER

Heavenly Father, thank You for Your desire to fill our lives with Your goodness and abundance. Help us to shift from a mindset of lack to a mindset of trust in You. Teach us to stay connected to You daily and to live with gratitude, contentment, and generosity. Let our lives overflow with Your presence and reflect Your goodness to others. In Jesus' name, Amen.

CHAPTER 2 STUDY GUIDE — TURNING SETBACKS INTO SUCCESS

A. SESSION AIM

To help participants understand that setbacks are a part of life but do not determine their destiny. This session will equip participants to respond to adversity by developing godly character through three key principles: fulfilling responsibilities, maintaining integrity, and trusting God's sovereignty.

B. ICE BREAKER

If you could go back and give your younger self advice during a difficult season, what would you say?

Leader Note: Keep responses light and optional. This allows reflection without putting pressure on anyone to share deeply personal experiences.

C. OPEN YOUR SESSION WITH PRAYER

Ask someone to lead in a prayer in their own words, or use the prayer below:

Heavenly Father, we thank You for bringing us together today. Open our hearts and minds to receive Your truth. Help us to trust You even in difficult seasons and to grow through every challenge we face. Strengthen our character and deepen our faith as we learn from Your Word. In Jesus' name, Amen.

D. INTRODUCTION (CHAPTER 2 SUMMARY)

Life is unpredictable, and many circumstances are beyond our control. Setbacks, disappointments, and unexpected challenges are part of the human experience. Yet, Scripture teaches that our success in life is not determined by our circumstances but by our character. The life of Joseph demonstrates that even when everything seems to go wrong—rejection, false accusation, and delay—God is still at work. Joseph's journey from the pit to the palace reveals that setbacks can become setups when we respond the right way. This session will show you how to navigate adversity by developing the kind of character that positions you for God's purpose and success.

E. BIBLE DISCUSSION

SECTION 1: PERSONALIZING THE MESSAGE

1. How do you typically respond when things don't go your way?

2. What is one setback that shaped your life in a significant way?

3. Do you believe challenges strengthen or weaken a person? Why?

4. What is harder for you—enduring difficulty or understanding its purpose?

SECTION 2: SCRIPTURE DISCOVERY

KEY POINT 1: Your Circumstances Do Not Define You—Your Character Does

Scriptures: Genesis 39:2–3; Proverbs 14:32

Scripture Insights: Joseph faced rejection, false accusation, and imprisonment, yet he remained faithful. His success was not rooted in favorable circumstances but in godly character. The difference-maker in life is not what happens to you, but how you respond.

Discussion Questions:

1. Read Genesis 39:2–3. What made Joseph successful despite his circumstances?

2. Why is it easy to blame circumstances for where we are in life?

3. Read Proverbs 14:32. How does integrity shape a person's future?

4. What character traits are most important during difficult seasons?

5. How can you grow your character when facing adversity?

KEY POINT 2: Fulfill Your Responsibilities Faithfully

Scriptures: Genesis 39:6, 22–23; Colossians 3:23

Scripture Insights: Joseph gave his best in every situation—whether in Potiphar's house or in prison. Faithfulness in small things leads to greater opportunities. God rewards diligence and responsibility.

Discussion Questions:

1. Read Colossians 3:23. What does it mean to work "as unto the Lord"?

2. Why is it difficult to stay faithful in unfavorable conditions?

3. Read Genesis 39:6, 22–23. How did Joseph demonstrate responsibility in difficult environments?

4. What area of your life requires greater diligence right now?

5. How can faithfulness today prepare you for future opportunities?

KEY POINT 3: Maintain Your Integrity at All Costs

Scriptures: Genesis 39:8–9; Proverbs 14:32

Scripture Insights: Joseph refused to compromise his integrity, even under pressure. Integrity protects your future and positions you for God's blessing. Short-term compromise leads to long-term consequences.

Discussion Questions:

1. Read Genesis 39:8–9. What motivated Joseph to resist temptation?

2. Why is integrity often tested during difficult seasons?

3. What are common areas where people compromise their integrity?

4. How does integrity protect your future?

5. What practical steps can you take to guard your character?

KEY POINT 4: Trust God's Sovereignty in Every Situation

Scriptures: Genesis 50:20; Romans 8:28

Scripture Insights: Joseph trusted that God was working behind the scenes, even when life didn't make sense. God has the power to turn what was meant for harm into something good. Trusting His sovereignty brings peace and confidence.

Discussion Questions:

1. Read Genesis 50:20. What does this verse teach about God's power?

2. Why is it difficult to trust God when circumstances are unclear?

3. Read Romans 8:28. How does this promise bring hope during setbacks?

4. How has God worked things out for good in your life before?

5. What situation do you need to surrender to God today?

KEY POINT 5: Setbacks Can Become Setups for Greater Purpose

Scriptures: Genesis 45:7–8; Proverbs 3:5–6

Scripture Insights: Joseph's setbacks positioned him to save nations. God often uses adversity to redirect and prepare us for greater impact. What looks like a delay may be divine preparation.

Discussion Questions:

1. Read Genesis 45:7–8. How did Joseph reinterpret his past?

2. Why do we often miss God's purpose in difficult moments?

3. Read Proverbs 3:5–6. What does it mean to trust God fully?

4. How can setbacks redirect your life toward God's purpose?

5. What is one way your current challenge might be preparing you?

F. SECTION 3: PERSONAL APPLICATION & REFLECTION

1. Which of the three principles (responsibility, integrity, trust) do you need to strengthen most?

2. What setback do you need to begin viewing through God's perspective?

3. What is one area where you need to remain faithful despite difficulty?

4. How can you intentionally trust God more in your current situation?

G. CLOSING WISDOM TAKE-AWAYS

1. Setbacks do not define your destiny—your character does.

2. Faithfulness and integrity position you for God's promotion.

3. What others mean for harm, God will use for your good and His purpose.

H. PRAYER

I. PRAYER POINTS

1. Ask God to strengthen your character during challenges

2. Pray for faithfulness and integrity in every area of life

3. Present your personal needs—asking God for wisdom, strength, and peace

4. Ask the Holy Spirit to help you trust God's plan fully

II. CLOSING PRAYER

Heavenly Father, thank You that our setbacks do not have the final word—You do. Help us to remain faithful, to guard our integrity, and to trust Your sovereignty in every situation. Strengthen our character and guide our steps so that we may walk in Your purpose. Use every challenge in our lives for good and for Your glory. In Jesus' name, Amen.

CHAPTER 3 STUDY GUIDE — HOW TO SEE YOUR DREAMS BECOME A REALITY

A. SESSION AIM

To equip participants with a clear, biblical process for turning God-given dreams into reality by applying the nine practical steps found in Genesis 24. This session will help participants gain clarity, strengthen faith, and take intentional, disciplined steps toward fulfilling their vision.

B. ICE BREAKER

Question: If you could spend one year fully focused on one goal or dream—with guaranteed success—what would you choose and why?

Leader Note: Keep responses light and encouraging. This question opens people up to thinking about focus and intentional living without pressure.

C. OPEN YOUR SESSION WITH PRAYER

Ask someone to lead in a prayer in their own words, or use the prayer below:

Heavenly Father, we thank You for bringing us together today. Open our hearts and minds to receive Your truth. Help us to trust the dreams You've placed within us and give us wisdom to pursue them according to Your will. Strengthen our faith, guide our steps, and let this time be transformational. In Jesus' name, Amen.

D. INTRODUCTION (CHAPTER 3 SUMMARY)

A focused life is a powerful life. Just as concentrated light can burn or cut through steel, a focused life aligned with God's purpose produces meaningful results. Many people have dreams but never see them fulfilled—not because they lack desire, but because they lack direction and disciplined focus. In Genesis 24, Abraham's servant provides a clear, biblical model for success. His mission reveals nine practical steps for turning vision into reality. This session will walk through those steps, helping you move from dreaming to doing, with God at the center of the process.

E. BIBLE DISCUSSION

SECTION 1: PERSONALIZING THE MESSAGE

1. What is one dream or goal you have thought about but have not fully pursued?

2. Do you tend to struggle more with clarity, action, or consistency? Why?

3. What usually stops people from following through on their dreams?

4. How would your life change if you became more focused and intentional?

SECTION 2: SCRIPTURE DISCOVERY

KEY POINT 1: Clarity Begins with Knowing Where You Are and What You Want

Scriptures: Genesis 24:1; Proverbs 29:18

Scripture Insights: Every meaningful journey begins with clarity. You must determine your current position and decide exactly what you want. Vague goals lead to vague results, but clear vision creates direction and momentum.

Discussion Questions:

1. Read Proverbs 29:18. Why is vision essential for a meaningful life?

2. Why is it important to assess your current position honestly?

3. What happens when goals are vague or undefined?

4. Which of the four questions (What do I want to be/do/have—and why?) challenges you the most?

5. How can clarity increase your motivation to pursue your goals?

KEY POINT 2: Your Dream Must Be Anchored in God's Promises and Prayer

Scriptures: Genesis 24:7, 12; James 4:2; Hebrews 4:16

Scripture Insights: Dreams become sustainable when they are anchored in God's Word and supported through prayer. God's promises give confidence, and prayer invites His power, guidance, and provision into the process.

Discussion Questions:

1. Read Genesis 24:7. How did God's promise give Abraham confidence?

2. Why is it important to attach God's promises to your goals?

3. Read James 4:2. What does this teach about asking God for help?

4. How does prayer reveal your dependence on God?

5. What is one specific area where you need to invite God more intentionally?

KEY POINT 3: You Must Identify Obstacles and Develop a Clear Plan

Scriptures: Genesis 24:15–24

Scripture Insights: Faith does not ignore reality—it acknowledges obstacles while trusting God. Identifying roadblocks and creating a step-by-step plan helps move vision into action.

Discussion Questions:

1. Why is it important to identify roadblocks instead of ignoring them?

2. What are some common barriers (emotional, financial, relational) people face?

3. How did Eliezer demonstrate strategic planning in his mission?

4. What are practical steps to break a large goal into manageable actions?

5. What is one obstacle you need to confront honestly?

KEY POINT 4: Progress Requires Patience, Persistence, and the Right People

Scriptures: Habakkuk 2:3; Ecclesiastes 4:12

Scripture Insights: Great dreams take time. Patience and persistence sustain progress, while the right relationships provide strength and support. Success is rarely achieved alone.

Discussion Questions:

1. Read Habakkuk 2:3. What does this teach about timing and patience?

2. Why do people often give up too soon?

3. How does persistence shape long-term success?

4. Read Ecclesiastes 4:12. Why is community essential?

5. Who are the people you need in your life to support your vision?

KEY POINT 5: Every Dream Requires Sacrifice and Commitment

Scripture: Genesis 24:53

Scripture Insights: There is always a cost attached to meaningful success. Time, energy, resources, and discipline are required. The question is not whether there is a price—but whether the dream is worth paying for.

Discussion Questions: Read Genesis 24:53

1. Why does every meaningful goal require sacrifice?

2. What are some common "costs" people must pay to succeed?

3. How do you determine if a goal is worth the cost?

4. What might you need to give up to move forward?

5. How can trusting God help you stay committed to the process?

F. SECTION 3: PERSONAL APPLICATION & REFLECTION

1. Which of the nine steps do you need to apply most urgently right now?

2. What is one specific goal you will begin to clarify this week?

3. What promise from God can you attach to your dream?

4. What is one practical step you will take toward your vision this week?

G. CLOSING WISDOM TAKE-AWAYS

1. Focus multiplies impact—what you concentrate on determines the significance of your life.

2. Clarity fuels progress—when you define your vision, you

activate your pursuit.

3. God's promises and your persistence turn dreams into reality.

H. PRAYER

I. PRAYER POINTS

1. Ask God for clarity and focus concerning your vision

2. Pray for discipline and persistence to follow through

3. Present your personal needs—asking God for wisdom, provision, and direction

4. Ask the Holy Spirit to guide your decisions and strengthen your faith

II. CLOSING PRAYER

Heavenly Father, thank You for the dreams You have placed within us. Help us to gain clarity, stay focused, and trust You through every step of the journey. Give us the discipline to act, the patience to endure, and the faith to believe Your promises. Surround us with the right people and strengthen us to pay the price required to fulfill Your purpose for our lives. In Jesus' name, Amen.

Chapter 4 Study Guide — How to Overcome the Enemy Within

A. SESSION AIM

To help participants identify and overcome the internal fears that hinder their life mission by applying biblical truths from the life of Moses. This session will equip participants to move forward in faith by embracing God's presence, character, power, and will.

B. ICE BREAKER

Question: If you had to try something new that pushes you slightly outside your comfort zone, what would it be?

Leader Note: Keep this light and forward-looking. The goal is to normalize growth and stepping out without pressure or fear of judgment.

C. OPEN YOUR SESSION WITH PRAYER

Ask someone to lead in a prayer in their own words, or use the prayer below:

Heavenly Father, we thank You for bringing us together today. Open our hearts and minds to receive Your truth. Help us to confront the fears that hold us back and replace them with faith in You. Give us courage to walk in our purpose and trust Your presence in every step. In Jesus' name, Amen.

D. INTRODUCTION (CHAPTER 4 SUMMARY)

Every person has a God-given purpose, yet many never fully step into it. The greatest barrier is not external opposition—it is internal fear. Fear of inadequacy, embarrassment, rejection, failure, and commitment can quietly sabotage our destiny. The life of Moses reveals that even those chosen by God wrestle with fear. Yet God provides a response for every fear. This session will help you identify the fears holding you back and replace them with faith rooted in God's presence, character, and promises—so you can move forward and fulfill your life mission.

E. BIBLE DISCUSSION

SECTION 1: PERSONALIZING THE MESSAGE

1. What is one fear that has held you back from doing something important?

2. Do you tend to avoid challenges or face them head-on? Why?

3. Which is harder for you—starting something new or staying committed to it?

4. What would you attempt if you were not afraid?

SECTION 2: SCRIPTURE DISCOVERY

KEY POINT 1: Overcome the Fear of Incompetence with God's Presence

Scripture: Exodus 3:11–12

Scripture Insights: Moses felt inadequate, but God's answer was simple: "I will be with you." Your calling is not based on your ability but on God's presence. When God is with you, your inadequacy is no longer a limitation.

Discussion Questions:

1. Read Exodus 3:11–12. What was Moses' concern, and how did God respond?

2. Why do we often focus on our limitations instead of God's power?

3. How does God's presence change your perspective on your abilities?

4. What is one area where you feel inadequate right now?

5. How can you rely more on God instead of yourself?

KEY POINT 2: Overcome the Fear of Embarrassment by Embracing God's Character

Scripture: Exodus 3:13–14

Scripture Insights: Moses feared being embarrassed or not having the right answers. God revealed His name: "I AM." Knowing who God is—eternal, unchanging, and true—gives us confidence to move forward.

Discussion Questions:

1. Read Exodus 3:13–14. Why was Moses concerned about what to say?

2. What does "I AM" reveal about God's nature?

3. How does knowing God's character reduce fear?

4. Why do we fear looking foolish or unprepared?

5. How can focusing on God instead of yourself increase confidence?

KEY POINT 3: Overcome the Fear of Rejection by Surrendering to God

Scripture: Exodus 4:1–4

Scripture Insights: Moses feared rejection, but God asked him to surrender what was in his hand. When we fully surrender our identity, influence, and resources to God, He uses them powerfully.

Discussion Questions:

1. Read Exodus 4:1–4. What did God ask Moses to do with his staff?

2. What does the staff represent in your own life?

3. Why do we fear rejection from others?

4. How does surrender shift your focus from people to God?

5. What is one thing you need to place fully in God's hands?

KEY POINT 4: Overcome the Fear of Comparison and Failure by Relying on God

Scripture: Exodus 4:10–12

Scripture Insights: Moses compared himself to others and felt inadequate. God reminded him that He is the source of ability. Your success is not determined by comparison, but by reliance on God.

Discussion Questions:

1. Read Exodus 4:10–12. What was Moses' excuse?

2. How does comparison affect confidence and action?

3. Why is perfectionism often rooted in fear?

4. What gifts has God given you that you may be overlooking?

5. How can trusting God help you move past fear of failure?

KEY POINT 5: Overcome the Fear of Commitment by Submitting to God's Will

Scripture: Exodus 4:13–14

Scripture Insights: Moses' final resistance was reluctance to commit. Fear often leads to avoidance. The breakthrough comes when we fully surrender to God's will and say "yes" to His calling.

Discussion Questions:

1. Read Exodus 4:13–14. What was Moses' final response to God?

2. Why do people resist committing to God's plan?

3. What are the risks of avoiding your calling?

4. What does full surrender to God look like?

5. What step of commitment is God asking you to take?

F. SECTION 3: PERSONAL APPLICATION & REFLECTION

1. Which of the five fears is most affecting your life right now?

2. What truth from this session speaks directly to that fear?

3. What is one "but" (excuse) you need to surrender to God?

4. What is one small step you will take this week despite fear?

G. CLOSING WISDOM TAKE-AWAYS

1. Fear is the enemy within—but God's presence is greater than every fear.

2. Your limitations do not disqualify you—God's power qualifies you.

3. Faith grows when you move forward, not when you wait for fear to disappear.

H. PRAYER

I. PRAYER POINTS

1. Ask God to reveal and remove the fears holding you back

2. Pray for courage to walk in your God-given purpose

3. Present your personal needs—asking God for strength, clarity, and confidence

4. Ask the Holy Spirit to fill you with faith, power, and boldness

II. CLOSING PRAYER

Heavenly Father, thank You that You have not given us a spirit of fear, but of power, love, and a sound mind. Help us to trust You more than our fears. Give us the courage to step forward in faith and to embrace the purpose You have for our lives. Teach us to rely on Your presence, surrender to Your will, and walk boldly in obedience. In Jesus' name, Amen.

CHAPTER 5 STUDY GUIDE — HOW TO BE CONFIDENT AND VICTORIOUS IN CRISIS

A. SESSION AIM

To help participants understand the nature of life's storms and learn how to respond with confidence by anchoring their lives in God's presence, purpose, and promises. This session will equip participants to remain steady, hopeful, and victorious in times of crisis.

B. ICE BREAKER

Question: When life gets stressful, what is one simple thing that helps you stay calm or regain focus?

Leader Note: Keep this practical and light. This helps participants connect everyday experiences with the idea of "anchors" in difficult moments.

C. OPEN YOUR SESSION WITH PRAYER

Ask someone to lead in a prayer in their own words, or use the prayer below:

Heavenly Father, we thank You for bringing us together today. Open our hearts and minds to receive Your truth. Help us to trust You in every storm we face and to find strength and confidence in Your presence. Teach us to stand firm and not lose hope in difficult times. In Jesus' name, Amen.

D. INTRODUCTION (CHAPTER 5 SUMMARY)

Life is filled with storms—unexpected challenges, hardships, and crises that can shake our confidence and test our faith. Some storms are self-inflicted, others are caused by people, and some are allowed by God for our growth. The story of Paul's shipwreck in Acts 27 shows us how quickly circumstances can spiral out of control—and how people often respond by drifting, discarding what matters, and eventually despairing. Yet Paul responded differently. He remained calm, confident, and anchored. This session will show you how to stand firm in life's storms by holding onto three unshakable anchors: God's presence, God's purpose, and God's promises.

E. BIBLE DISCUSSION

SECTION 1: PERSONALIZING THE MESSAGE

1. What kind of "storm" are you currently facing (or have recently faced)?

2. When pressure increases, do you tend to stay focused or feel overwhelmed?

3. Have you ever made a decision during a difficult time that you later regretted?

4. What usually gives you hope when things feel uncertain?

SECTION 2: SCRIPTURE DISCOVERY

KEY POINT 1: Understand the Causes of Life's Storms

Scriptures: Acts 27:9–13; Proverbs 14:12

Scripture Insights: Storms can come from poor decisions, following the wrong voices, or relying on circumstances instead of God. Understanding their causes helps us avoid unnecessary hardship.

Discussion Questions:

1. Read Acts 27:9–13. What mistakes led the sailors into trouble?

2. Why is it dangerous to follow the wrong "experts"?

3. How can popular opinion lead us in the wrong direction?

4. Why can circumstances be misleading?

5. What steps can you take to seek God's direction before making decisions?

KEY POINT 2: Recognize How Storms Affect You

Scriptures: Acts 27:15–20

Scripture Insights: Storms often cause people to drift from their purpose, discard important values, and fall into despair. Recognizing these patterns helps us respond differently.

Discussion Questions:

1. Read Acts 27:15–20. What happened to the sailors during the storm?

2. What does it mean to "drift" spiritually or emotionally?

3. What are some things people tend to "throw overboard" during crisis?

4. Why is despair so dangerous?

5. How can you guard your faith during difficult seasons?

KEY POINT 3: Anchor Your Life in God's Presence

Scriptures: Acts 27:22–23; Hebrews 13:5

Scripture Insights: God's presence is your first anchor. No matter how intense the storm, God is with you. His presence brings peace, strength, and confidence.

Discussion Questions:

1. Read Acts 27:22–23. Why was Paul confident in the storm?

2. How does knowing God is with you change your perspective?

3. Read Hebrews 13:5. What promise does God give?

4. Why do we sometimes feel like God is distant during hardship?

5. How can you become more aware of God's presence daily?

KEY POINT 4: Anchor Your Life in God's Purpose

Scriptures: Acts 27:24; Jeremiah 29:11

Scripture Insights: Storms cannot cancel God's purpose for your life. Even setbacks and delays are part of His greater plan. Your destiny is secure in Him.

Discussion Questions:

1. Read Acts 27:24. What did God reveal about Paul's future?

2. How does knowing God has a plan bring confidence?

3. Read Jeremiah 29:11. What does this promise mean to you?

4. Why is it easy to focus on problems instead of purpose?

5. How can you stay focused on God's purpose during trials?

KEY POINT 5: Anchor Your Life in God's Promises

Scriptures: Acts 27:25; Hebrews 6:18–19

Scripture Insights: God's promises are unbreakable. Faith in His Word provides stability and hope, even when everything else feels uncertain.

Discussion Questions:

1. Read Acts 27:25. What gave Paul confidence?

2. Why is trusting God's promises essential in crisis?

3. Read Hebrews 6:18–19. What does it mean that hope is an anchor?

4. How can you strengthen your faith in God's promises?

5. What promise from God do you need to hold onto right now?

F. SECTION 3: PERSONAL APPLICATION & REFLECTION

1. Which type of storm are you currently experiencing?

2. How are you responding—drifting, discarding, or standing firm?

3. Which "anchor" (presence, purpose, or promises) do you need most right now?

4. What is one practical step you will take to stay grounded in your faith this week?

G. CLOSING WISDOM TAKE-AWAYS

1. **Storms are inevitable—but defeat is optional when you are anchored in God.**

2. **God's presence calms you, His purpose guides you, and His promises secure you.**

3. **You may lose the ship—but with God, you will never lose your life or your destiny.**

H. PRAYER

I. PRAYER POINTS

1. Ask God for strength and confidence in your current storm

2. Pray for wisdom to make decisions aligned with His will

3. Present your personal needs—asking God for peace, provision, and direction

4. Ask the Holy Spirit to anchor your heart in God's truth

II. CLOSING PRAYER

Heavenly Father, thank You that You are with us in every storm. Help us to trust You when life feels uncertain and to anchor our lives in Your presence, purpose, and promises. Strengthen our faith so that we do not drift, despair, or lose hope. Give us confidence that no matter what we face, You will bring us through. In Jesus' name, Amen.

Chapter 6 Study Guide—How to Break Free from Strongholds

A. SESSION AIM

To help participants understand the nature of strongholds and equip them with biblical steps to break free from destructive habits and thought patterns. This session will guide participants to rely on God's power, take personal responsibility, and pursue lasting transformation through practical spiritual disciplines.

B. ICE BREAKER

Question: If you could instantly replace one unhelpful habit with a positive one, what would it be?

Leader Note: Keep this light and judgment-free. This allows participants to engage without feeling exposed or pressured.

C. OPEN YOUR SESSION WITH PRAYER

Ask someone to lead in a prayer in their own words, or use the prayer below:

Heavenly Father, we thank You for bringing us together today. Open our hearts and minds to receive Your truth. Help us to recognize the areas where we need freedom and give us the courage to surrender those areas to You. Strengthen us by Your Spirit to walk in victory and transformation. In Jesus' name, Amen.

D. INTRODUCTION (CHAPTER 6 SUMMARY)

Strongholds are patterns of thinking and behavior that trap us and keep us from living the life God intends. Like a plane grounded by a storm, strongholds prevent forward movement no matter how much we desire change. These struggles may be visible, like addiction, or hidden, like fear, pride, or insecurity. Scripture teaches that we are in a spiritual battle, and victory does not come through human effort alone but through God's power. This session will introduce a practical, biblical pathway to freedom using the B–R–E–A–K F–R–E–E framework—helping you move from bondage to lasting transformation.

E. BIBLE DISCUSSION

SECTION 1: PERSONALIZING THE MESSAGE

> 1. What is one habit or pattern you've struggled to change?
>
> 2. Why do you think some habits are so difficult to break?
>
> 3. Do you tend to deal with struggles privately or seek help? Why?
>
> 4. What does "freedom" look like in your life right now?

SECTION 2: SCRIPTURE DISCOVERY

KEY POINT 1: Take Immediate Responsibility for Change

Scriptures: Ecclesiastes 11:4; Proverbs 19:3

Scripture Insights: Freedom begins when you take ownership. Delaying change or blaming others strengthens the stronghold. Real transformation starts when you say, "This is my responsibility, and I will act today."

Discussion Questions:

> 1. Read Ecclesiastes 11:4. Why is waiting for the "right time" dangerous?

2. How does blame-shifting prevent growth?

3. Why is personal responsibility essential for change?

4. What excuses have you used that may be holding you back?

5. What step can you take today instead of delaying?

KEY POINT 2: Examine Your Life Honestly

Scriptures: Lamentations 3:40; Psalm 32:3–5

Scripture Insights: You cannot change what you refuse to confront. Honest self-examination exposes the root of strongholds and opens the door for healing and transformation.

Discussion Questions:

1. Read Lamentations 3:40. What does it mean to "examine your ways"?

2. Why do people avoid honest self-reflection?

3. Read Psalm 32:3–5. What happened when David stopped hiding?

4. How does honesty lead to freedom?

5. What area of your life needs honest evaluation?

KEY POINT 3: Surrender Control to Christ

Scriptures: Romans 6:12–13; Colossians 1:17

Scripture Insights: Lasting change requires surrender. Freedom comes when Christ is not just part of your life but in control of your life. His power enables what human effort cannot achieve.

Discussion Questions:

1. Read Romans 6:12–13. What does it mean to give yourself completely to God?

2. Why is partial surrender ineffective?

3. What does it look like for Christ to be "in control" of your life?

4. What competes with God for control in your life?

5. What would full surrender look like for you this week?

KEY POINT 4: Guard Your Environment and Your Mind

Scriptures: Proverbs 4:23; Philippians 4:8

Scripture Insights: Strongholds are reinforced by what we allow into our minds and environments. Freedom requires intentional boundaries and replacing harmful thoughts with God's truth.

Discussion Questions:

1. Read Proverbs 4:23. Why is guarding your heart so important?

2. What are common triggers that lead to temptation?

3. Read Philippians 4:8. What should we focus our minds on?

4. How does replacing thoughts lead to transformation?

5. What is one boundary you need to set to avoid temptation?

KEY POINT 5: Pursue Freedom Through Community and Purpose

Scriptures: James 5:16; Ecclesiastes 4:9–10

Scripture Insights: Freedom is not a solo journey. Confession, accountability, and community provide strength and support. God also uses your healing to help others.

Discussion Questions:

1. Read James 5:16. Why is confession important for healing?

2. Why do people struggle to ask for help?

3. Read Ecclesiastes 4:9–10. What is the benefit of community?

4. How can your story help someone else?

5. Who can you trust to walk with you in your journey?

F. SECTION 3: PERSONAL APPLICATION & REFLECTION

1. Which step in the BREAK FREE process do you need most right now?

2. What stronghold do you need to confront honestly?

3. What is one boundary or change you will implement this week?

4. Who will you invite to support and pray for you?

G. CLOSING WISDOM TAKE-AWAYS

1. Strongholds lose power when truth replaces deception and surrender replaces control.

2. You cannot break free alone—God's power and community are essential for lasting change.

3. Freedom begins the moment you take responsibility and surrender your life fully to Christ.

H. PRAYER

I. PRAYER POINTS

1. Ask God to reveal and break every stronghold in your life

2. Pray for strength to walk in discipline and obedience

3. Present your personal needs—asking God for healing, freedom, and renewal

4. Ask the Holy Spirit to guide and empower your transformation

II. CLOSING PRAYER

Heavenly Father, thank You that freedom is possible through You. Help us to recognize the strongholds in our lives and give us the courage to confront them. Teach us to surrender fully to You and to rely on Your power daily. Surround us with the right people and help us walk in truth, discipline, and victory. In Jesus' name, Amen.

Chapter 7 Study Guide—What It Takes to Be a Great Leader

The 8 Cs of Influential Leadership

A. SESSION AIM

To help participants understand that leadership is influence rooted in character and to develop the eight essential qualities of influential leadership modeled in the life of Nehemiah. This session will challenge participants to grow intentionally in their leadership and fulfill their God-given assignment.

B. ICE BREAKER

Question: What is one quality you appreciate most in a leader—and how has it impacted you?

Leader Note: Keep responses simple and positive. This helps participants connect leadership with real-life influence.

C. OPEN YOUR SESSION WITH PRAYER

Ask someone to lead in a prayer in their own words, or use the prayer below:

Heavenly Father, we thank You for bringing us together today. Open our hearts and minds to receive Your truth. Teach us how to lead with character, wisdom, and courage. Help us to influence others in a way that honors You and advances Your purpose. In Jesus' name, Amen.

D. INTRODUCTION (CHAPTER 7 SUMMARY)

Nothing significant happens without leadership. Throughout history, progress has always followed those willing to step up and take responsibility. Biblical leadership is not about titles or positions—it is about influence grounded in character. Nehemiah provides a powerful example of this kind of leadership. Faced with overwhelming challenges, opposition, and responsibility, he demonstrated eight essential qualities that enabled him to rebuild a broken nation. This session will explore the "8 Cs of Influential Leadership" and help you grow into the leader God has called you to be.

E. BIBLE DISCUSSION

SECTION 1: PERSONALIZING THE MESSAGE

1. In what areas of your life are you currently influencing others?

2. Do you view yourself as a leader? Why or why not?

3. What leadership quality do you find most challenging to develop?

4. What kind of impact do you want your life to have on others?

SECTION 2: SCRIPTURE DISCOVERY

KEY POINT 1: Compassion — Care Deeply About People

Scripture: Nehemiah 1:4

Scripture Insights: Leadership begins with love. Nehemiah's compassion moved him to action. Influential leaders genuinely care about people and are motivated by their well-being.

Discussion Questions:

1. Read Nehemiah 1:4. How did Nehemiah respond to the people's situation?

2. Why is compassion essential for leadership?

3. How does caring for people build influence?

4. What happens when leaders lack compassion?

5. How can you demonstrate compassion this week?

KEY POINT 2: Contemplation — Seek God Before Acting

Scripture: Nehemiah 1:5–6

Scripture Insights: Great leaders spend time with God. Nehemiah prayed, reflected, and sought wisdom before making decisions. Private devotion strengthens public leadership.

Discussion Questions:

1. Why is prayer essential for leadership decisions?

2. How does reflection improve decision-making?

3. What happens when leaders act without thinking?

4. How can you create space for contemplation daily?

5. What decision do you need to bring before God?

KEY POINT 3: Cheerfulness — Maintain a Positive Spirit

Scripture: Nehemiah 8:10

Scripture Insights: Leaders set the emotional tone. Nehemiah's cheerfulness encouraged others even during difficulty. Joy strengthens people and fuels momentum.

Discussion Questions:

1. Read Nehemiah 8:10. Why is joy a source of strength?

2. How does attitude affect leadership influence?

3. Why do people follow positive leaders?

4. What drains your joy?

5. How can you cultivate a more encouraging attitude?

KEY POINT 4: Concentration — Stay Focused on the Mission

Scripture: Nehemiah 6:3–4

Scripture Insights: Great leaders remain focused and avoid distractions. Nehemiah refused to be pulled away from his assignment. Focus leads to progress and success.

Discussion Questions:

1. Read Nehemiah 6:3–4. How did Nehemiah handle distractions?

2. Why is focus essential for success?

3. What are common distractions in leadership?

4. How can you stay focused on your priorities?

5. What is one distraction you need to eliminate?

KEY POINT 5: Creativity — Solve Problems with Innovation

Scripture: Nehemiah 4:13–18

Scripture Insights: Leaders think creatively and adapt to challenges. Nehemiah found innovative ways to protect and motivate his people while accomplishing the mission.

Discussion Questions:

1. How did Nehemiah demonstrate creative problem-solving?

2. Why is creativity important in leadership?

3. How can challenges inspire innovation?

4. What problem do you need to approach differently?

5. How can you develop creative thinking?

KEY POINT 6: Courage — Act Despite Fear

Scripture: Nehemiah 2:4–5

Scripture Insights: Courage is moving forward despite fear. Nehemiah took bold steps even when the risks were high. Leadership requires stepping outside comfort zones.

Discussion Questions:

1. What risks did Nehemiah take?

2. Why is courage necessary for leadership?

3. What fears hold people back from leading?

4. What step of faith is God calling you to take?

5. How can you grow in courage?

KEY POINT 7: Clear Conscience — Lead with Integrity

Scripture: Nehemiah 5:14–15

Scripture Insights: Integrity is the foundation of lasting leadership. Nehemiah refused to abuse power and remained accountable to God.

Discussion Questions:

1. Why is integrity essential for leadership?

2. How does integrity build trust?

3. What are common temptations leaders face?

4. How can you guard your integrity daily?

5. What area of your life needs greater accountability?

KEY POINT 8: Conviction — Stand Firm in Your Calling

Scripture: Galatians 6:9

Scripture Insights: Conviction keeps leaders steady under pressure. Nehemiah remained committed despite opposition. Strong beliefs sustain long-term success.

Discussion Questions:

1. Why is conviction important in leadership?

2. How did Nehemiah handle opposition?

3. What pressures can weaken conviction?

4. What do you stand for as a leader?

5. How can you strengthen your convictions?

F. SECTION 3: PERSONAL APPLICATION & REFLECTION

1. Which of the 8 Cs is strongest in your life right now?

2. Which leadership quality do you need to develop most?

3. What is one action you will take this week to grow as a leader?

4. Who is one person you can intentionally influence this week?

G. CLOSING WISDOM TAKE-AWAYS

1. Leadership is influence built on character, not position or personality.

2. Great leaders are formed in private through prayer, integrity, and discipline.

3. When you stand firm in your convictions, God will empower your influence.

H. PRAYER

I. PRAYER POINTS

1. Ask God to develop your character as a leader

2. Pray for wisdom, focus, and courage

3. Present your personal needs—asking God for strength and direction

4. Ask the Holy Spirit to help you influence others for His purpose

II. CLOSING PRAYER

Heavenly Father, thank You for calling us to lead and influence others. Help us to grow in character, wisdom, and courage. Teach us to lead with compassion, integrity, and conviction. Strengthen us to remain faithful to Your calling and to make a positive impact in every area of our lives. In Jesus' name, Amen.

CHAPTER 8 STUDY GUIDE — HOW TO LIVE A LIFE OF SIGNIFICANCE

A. SESSION AIM

To help participants understand that a life of significance is not determined by background or ability, but by great ambition, growing faith, and a genuine prayer life. This session will challenge participants to think bigger, trust God more deeply, and pursue a life that makes a lasting impact.

B. ICE BREAKER

Question: If you could make a positive impact in one area of the world (family, community, career, or ministry), what would it be?

Leader Note: Keep responses light and aspirational. This helps participants begin thinking about purpose and influence without pressure.

C. OPEN YOUR SESSION WITH PRAYER

Ask someone to lead in a prayer in their own words, or use the prayer below:

Heavenly Father, we thank You for bringing us together today. Open our hearts and minds to receive Your truth. Help us to see the purpose You have for our lives and give us the courage to pursue it. Strengthen our faith and deepen our desire to live a life that honors You. In Jesus' name, Amen.

D. INTRODUCTION (CHAPTER 8 SUMMARY)

Every person desires to live a life that matters. Yet many settle for mediocrity, limited by fear, labels, or small thinking. The story of Jabez shows us that significance is not reserved for the extraordinary—it is available to anyone who dares to believe God. In just two verses, Jabez stands out among hundreds because of his ambition, faith, and prayer. He refused to be defined by his past and boldly asked God to enlarge his life. This session will help you break free from limiting beliefs and step into a life of significance by embracing God's purpose for you.

E. BIBLE DISCUSSION

SECTION 1: PERSONALIZING THE MESSAGE

> 1. What does a "life of significance" mean to you?
>
> 2. Do you feel you are currently living below your potential? Why or why not?
>
> 3. What fears or limitations have held you back from dreaming bigger?
>
> 4. What would you attempt if you fully trusted God?

SECTION 2: SCRIPTURE DISCOVERY

KEY POINT 1: You Need Great Ambition

Scripture: 1 Chronicles 4:10

Scripture Insights: Jabez refused to settle for an average life. He boldly asked God to enlarge his territory. A life of significance begins with a willingness to dream big and trust God for more.

Discussion Questions:

> 1. Read 1 Chronicles 4:10. What does Jabez ask God for?

2. Why do many people settle for average living?

3. What are common misconceptions about ambition?

4. How can ambition be aligned with God's will?

5. What "bigger vision" is God calling you to pursue?

KEY POINT 2: You Need a Growing Faith

Scripture: Romans 10:17

Scripture Insights: Jabez's life was not defined by his limitations but by his faith. God uses ordinary people who believe Him for extraordinary things. Faith unlocks potential beyond circumstances.

Discussion Questions:

1. Why is faith more important than ability?

2. How do labels and past experiences limit people?

3. Read Romans 10:17. How does faith grow?

4. What mindset keeps people from trusting God fully?

5. How can you strengthen your faith daily?

KEY POINT 3: You Need a Genuine Prayer Life

Scripture: Jeremiah 33:3

Scripture Insights: Jabez's prayer was the turning point in his life. A consistent, sincere prayer life invites God's power, presence, and protection into every area of life.

Discussion Questions:

1. Why was Jabez's prayer so significant?

2. What does it mean to pray with intention and faith?

3. Read Jeremiah 33:3. What promise does God give?

4. How can prayer shape your future?

5. What specific prayers do you need to begin praying?

KEY POINT 4: Ask for God's Power

Scripture: Ephesians 3:20

Scripture Insights: Jabez asked for God's blessing and expansion. God's power enables us to accomplish what we cannot do on our own.

Discussion Questions:

1. Why is it important to ask God boldly?

2. What limits people from asking God for more?

3. Read Ephesians 3:20. What does this reveal about God's ability?

4. How can your prayers become more specific?

5. What is one bold request you need to bring to God?

KEY POINT 5: Depend on God's Presence and Protection

Scriptures: 1 Chronicles 4:10; Psalm 3:3

Scripture Insights: Jabez asked for God's presence and protection, knowing that growth brings greater responsibility and opposition. A significant life requires dependence on God daily.

Discussion Questions:

1. Why did Jabez ask for God's presence?

2. How does God's presence provide confidence?

3. Why is protection important as influence grows?

4. Read Psalm 3:3. What does God promise to be for us?

5. How can you rely more on God in your daily life?

F. SECTION 3: PERSONAL APPLICATION & REFLECTION

1. What is one area where you need to think bigger and trust God more?

2. What label or limitation do you need to release?

3. What is one specific prayer you will begin praying daily?

4. What step can you take this week toward a life of significance?

G. CLOSING WISDOM TAKE-AWAYS

1. A life of significance begins when you dare to believe God for more.

2. Your past does not define you—your faith and prayer determine your future.

3. God's power, presence, and protection enable you to live beyond average.

H. PRAYER

I. PRAYER POINTS

1. Ask God to expand your vision and ambition

2. Pray for increased faith and trust in Him

3. Present your personal needs—asking God for direction and strength

4. Ask the Holy Spirit to guide you into a life of purpose and significance

II. CLOSING PRAYER

Heavenly Father, thank You for calling us to live a life of significance. Help us to think bigger, believe deeper, and pray with boldness. Remove every limitation and give us the courage to pursue Your purpose. Let our lives reflect Your power, presence, and glory. In Jesus' name, Amen.

CHAPTER 9 STUDY GUIDE — HOW TO OVERCOME YOUR WEAKNESS TO BECOME A STRONGER PERSON

A. SESSION AIM

To help participants recognize the habits and attitudes that weaken their lives and learn how to overcome them through discipline, forgiveness, and faithful commitment. This session will equip participants to rely on God's strength and finish strong in their purpose.

B. ICE BREAKER

Question: What is one positive habit you've developed that has made your life better?

Leader Note: Keep this encouraging and practical. This helps participants connect the idea of discipline with real-life growth.

C. OPEN YOUR SESSION WITH PRAYER

Ask someone to lead in a prayer in their own words, or use the prayer below:

Heavenly Father, we thank You for bringing us together today. Open our hearts and minds to receive Your truth. Help us to recognize areas of weakness and give us the strength to overcome them. Teach us to rely on Your power and to grow into the people You have called us to be. In

Jesus' name, Amen.

D. INTRODUCTION (CHAPTER 9 SUMMARY)

Many people begin life with great potential but lose strength along the way. Like a marathon runner who starts strong but fades before the finish, weakness can slowly drain our energy and derail our purpose. The life of Samson shows how even a strong person can become weak through poor choices. His downfall was not due to lack of ability but to undisciplined living, resentment, and carelessness. Yet his story also reveals God's grace and the possibility of restoration. This session will help you identify the patterns that weaken your life and apply biblical principles to become stronger and finish well.

E. BIBLE DISCUSSION

SECTION 1: PERSONALIZING THE MESSAGE

1. What area of your life do you feel needs strengthening right now?

2. Do you find it easier to start strong or stay consistent over time?

3. What tends to drain your energy the most—emotionally, spiritually, or mentally?

4. What does "finishing strong" mean to you?

SECTION 2: SCRIPTURE DISCOVERY

KEY POINT 1: An Undisciplined Lifestyle Will Weaken You

Scriptures: Judges 14:1–3; Galatians 6:7–8

Scripture Insights: Samson repeatedly chose pleasure over principles, allowing his desires to control his decisions. A lack of self-discipline leads to long-term consequences and spiritual weakness.

Discussion Questions:

1. Read Judges 14:1–3. What kind of decisions was Samson

making?

2. Why is it dangerous to live based on feelings instead of principles?

3. Read Galatians 6:7–8. What does it mean to reap what you sow?

4. What areas of your life require greater discipline?

5. How can you begin to choose principles over pleasure?

KEY POINT 2: Resentment Will Weaken You

Scriptures: Judges 15:7; Proverbs 14:29

Scripture Insights: Samson allowed anger and revenge to control his actions. Resentment drains emotional and spiritual strength and keeps us stuck in the past.

Discussion Questions:

1. How did Samson respond when he was hurt?

2. Why is resentment so destructive?

3. Read Proverbs 14:29. What does it say about controlling anger?

4. How does unforgiveness affect your life?

5. Who or what do you need to release to God today?

KEY POINT 3: Carelessness Will Weaken You

Scriptures: Judges 16:15–17; 1 Corinthians 10:12

Scripture Insights: Samson's downfall came through small compromises that led to major failure. Carelessness in commitments opens the door to destruction.

Discussion Questions:

1. Read Judges 16:15–17. What led to Samson's downfall?

2. Why are small compromises dangerous?

3. Read 1 Corinthians 10:12. What warning does this give?

4. Where are you tempted to be careless in your life?

KEY POINT 4: Discipline Your Desires to Grow Stronger

Scripture: 1 Peter 4:1–2

Scripture Insights: Strength comes from self-control and living according to God's will rather than human desires. Discipline builds lasting strength and stability.

Discussion Questions:

1. Read 1 Peter 4:1–2. What does it mean to live for God's will?

2. Why is self-discipline essential for growth?

3. What habits help strengthen your spiritual life?

4. How can you train yourself to say "no" to unhealthy desires?

5. What is one discipline you need to develop?

KEY POINT 5: Finish Strong by Honoring Your Commitments

Scriptures: Ecclesiastes 7:8; 1 Corinthians 15:58

Scripture Insights: Samson's life reminds us that starting well is not enough—we must finish well. Honoring commitments, even when difficult, leads to lasting strength and impact.

Discussion Questions:

1. Read Ecclesiastes 7:8. Why is the end better than the beginning?

2. Why do people struggle to finish what they start?

3. Read 1 Corinthians 15:58. What does it mean to remain steadfast?

4. What commitments do you need to renew?

5. How can you stay strong through challenges?

F. SECTION 3: PERSONAL APPLICATION & REFLECTION

1. Which of the three weaknesses (undisciplined living, resentment, carelessness) affects you most?

2. What is one habit you need to change immediately?

3. What relationship needs healing or forgiveness?

4. What commitment do you need to honor moving forward?

G. CLOSING WISDOM TAKE-AWAYS

1. Weakness grows when discipline fades—but strength grows when you live by God's principles.

2. Resentment drains your strength—release it so you can move forward.

3. Finishing strong requires faithfulness, not just a good start.

H. PRAYER

I. PRAYER POINTS

1. Ask God to strengthen you in areas of weakness

2. Pray for discipline, self-control, and wisdom

3. Present your personal needs—asking God for healing and renewal

4. Ask the Holy Spirit to help you remain faithful and finish strong

II. CLOSING PRAYER

Heavenly Father, thank You that our strength comes from You. Help us to overcome every weakness that holds us back. Give us discipline to live by Your principles, grace to release resentment, and faithfulness to honor our commitments. Strengthen us to finish strong and fulfill the purpose You have for our lives. In Jesus' name, Amen.

Chapter 10 Study Guide — How to Recover from Your Hurts

A. SESSION AIM

To help participants understand how to recover from life's wounds by turning to God, processing their pain honestly, and applying biblical steps toward healing. This session will guide participants to find strength, hope, and restoration through God's presence and promises.

B. ICE BREAKER

Question: When you're going through a tough time, what helps you feel encouraged or supported?

Leader Note: Keep this light and open-ended. This allows participants to engage without needing to share deeply personal pain upfront.

C. OPEN YOUR SESSION WITH PRAYER

Ask someone to lead in a prayer in their own words, or use the prayer below:

Heavenly Father, we thank You for bringing us together today. Open our hearts and minds to receive Your truth. You see every hurt and every burden we carry. Help us to bring our pain to You and trust You for healing, strength, and restoration. In Jesus' name, Amen.

D. INTRODUCTION (CHAPTER 10 SUMMARY)

Life is filled with pain, loss, and unexpected hardship. No one escapes being wounded—physically, emotionally, or spiritually. The difference between those who recover and those who remain stuck often lies in how they respond to their pain. The life of Job shows us that even in the deepest suffering, it is possible to remain faithful and experience restoration. God invites us to turn to Him in our brokenness, not away from Him. This session will provide practical, biblical steps to help you process your pain and move toward healing and renewal.

E. BIBLE DISCUSSION

SECTION 1: PERSONALIZING THE MESSAGE

1. When you go through a difficult time, do you tend to open up or withdraw?

2. What is one type of hurt people commonly struggle to recover from?

3. Why do you think some people bounce back while others stay stuck?

4. What does healing look like to you?

SECTION 2: SCRIPTURE DISCOVERY

KEY POINT 1: Tell God Your Feelings Honestly

Scriptures: 1 Peter 5:7; Psalm 55:22

Scripture Insights: Healing begins with honesty. God invites us to bring our pain, anger, fear, and grief to Him. Expressing our feelings to God is an act of faith, not weakness.

Discussion Questions:

1. Read 1 Peter 5:7. What does it mean to "cast your cares" on God?

2. Why do people struggle to express their true feelings?

3. How can suppressing emotions affect your health and faith?

4. What emotions are hardest for you to bring to God?

5. How can honesty deepen your relationship with God?

KEY POINT 2: Praise God Despite Your Circumstances

Scriptures: Job 1:21–22; Habakkuk 3:17–18

Scripture Insights: True faith is revealed when we praise God in difficult times. Praise shifts our focus from our pain to God's power and goodness.

Discussion Questions:

1. Read Job 1:21–22. How did Job respond to loss?

2. Why is praising God during hardship difficult?

3. Read Habakkuk 3:17–18. What does it mean to choose joy?

4. How does praise strengthen your faith?

5. What can you thank God for even in your current situation?

KEY POINT 3: Ask God for Wisdom and Strength

Scriptures: James 1:5; Psalm 37:39

Scripture Insights: When we are hurting, we need wisdom to know what to do and strength to carry it out. God promises to provide both when we ask.

Discussion Questions:

1. Read James 1:5. What does God promise to give?

2. Why is it important to seek God's wisdom during pain?

3. How can emotions lead us in the wrong direction?

4. What strength do you need from God right now?

5. How can you rely on God instead of your feelings?

KEY POINT 4: Gather with Others for Support

Scriptures: Hebrews 10:24–25; Psalm 63:2

Scripture Insights: Healing happens in community. Isolation deepens pain, but connection with others brings encouragement, strength, and hope.

Discussion Questions:

1. Why do people isolate themselves when they are hurting?

2. Read Hebrews 10:24–25. Why is community important?

3. How can others help you through difficult times?

4. Who can you turn to for support?

5. How can you be a source of support for others?

KEY POINT 5: Keep Persisting and Trust God

Scriptures: Revelation 14:12; 1 Peter 5:10

Scripture Insights: Healing takes time. God calls us to endure, trust Him, and keep moving forward. Persistence leads to restoration and strength.

Discussion Questions:

1. Why is it difficult to keep going during pain?

2. Read 1 Peter 5:10. What does God promise after suffering?

3. How does hope help you endure hardship?

4. What does it mean to "not give up"?

5. What helps you stay strong during long seasons of difficulty?

F. SECTION 3: PERSONAL APPLICATION & REFLECTION

1. What hurt do you need to bring honestly before God?

2. What is one way you can practice praise this week?

3. What wisdom or strength do you need to ask God for?

4. Who can you connect with for support and encouragement?

G. CLOSING WISDOM TAKE-AWAYS

1. Healing begins when you bring your pain honestly to God.

2. Praise in the midst of pain is a declaration of trust in God's goodness.

3. Persistence through hardship positions you for God's restoration.

H. PRAYER

I. PRAYER POINTS

1. Ask God to heal your heart and restore your strength

2. Pray for faith to trust Him in difficult times

3. Present your personal needs—asking God for comfort, wisdom, and peace

4. Ask the Holy Spirit to help you remain strong and hopeful

II. CLOSING PRAYER

Heavenly Father, thank You that You are close to the brokenhearted and that You heal our wounds. Help us to trust You in our pain and to bring every hurt before You. Strengthen us to endure, guide us with Your wisdom, and surround us with support. Restore our hearts and renew our hope as we walk with You. In Jesus' name, Amen.

Other Books

By

Mike Prah

HIDDEN NO MORE: THE SECRETS GOD REVEALS

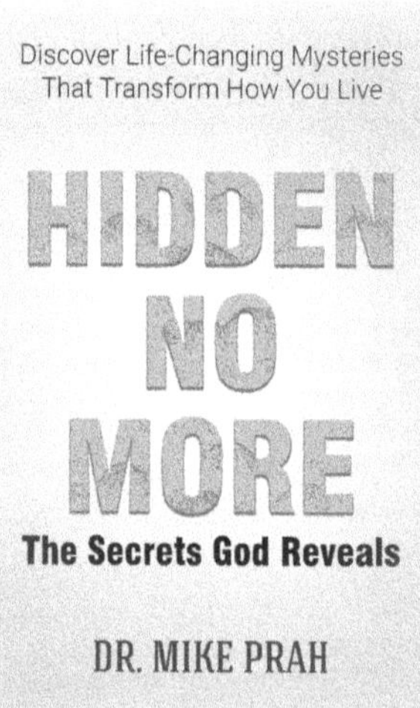

What if the answers to life's deepest questions were never meant to stay hidden?

Hidden No More: The Secrets God Reveals explores the mysteries once hidden in God's redemptive plan but now revealed through Jesus Christ. Through twelve powerful biblical "secrets," Mike Prah shows how God's truth brings clarity, inspires transformation, strengthens faith in hardship, and anchors lasting hope for living with purpose and confidence.

The secrets are no longer hidden. Live in the light of what God has revealed.

Available in Hardcover, Paperback, E-Book, and Audio Book. Get your copy at:

http://mikeprah.com/bookstore

Also available at Amazon.com, BarnesandNobles.com, Books-a-Million, Walmart.com and several online bookstores, Audio books, and E-book retailers world-wide including Kindle, Apple Books, Google Books. For bulk purchases contact: info@mikeprah.com.

You Are Unstoppable: Practical Principles for Overcoming Setbacks and Experiencing Breakthroughs

DISCOVER HOW TO OVERCOME life's obstacles and step into your God-given destiny. In *You Are Unstoppable*, Mike Prah shares empowering biblical truths, inspiring stories, and practical strategies to help you experience breakthrough and live with purpose. Step into your calling—because with God, you are truly unstoppable!

Available in Hardcover, Paperback, E-Book, and Audio Book at

http://mikeprah.com/bookstore

Also available at Amazon.com, BarnesandNobles.com, Books-a-Million, Walmart.com and several online bookstores, Audio books, and E-book retailers world-wide including Kindle, Apple Books, Google Books. For bulk purchases contact: info@mikeprah.com.

40 Days of Hope in Grief and Loss: A Devotional

If you're navigating the pain of grief, this 40-day devotional offers heartfelt encouragement through Scripture, real-life stories, and prayers. Mike Prah gently guides readers to find comfort, strength, and renewed hope in God's presence. Whether your loss is recent or long past, this book is a healing journey toward joy, purpose, and peace.

Available in Hardback from http://mikeprah.com/bookstore

Also available at Amazon.com, BarnesandNobles.com, Books-a-Million, Walmart.com and several online bookstores and E-book retailers world-wide.

For bulk purchases contact info@mikeprah.com

7 Secrets of Leaders Who Last

7 SECRETS OF LEADERS WHO LAST equips pastors, ministry leaders, and servant-leaders to overcome the most common traps that derail leadership and embrace the habits that ensure longevity. Packed with a practical message outline, key takeaways, group discussion guide, and a 14-day devotional, this resource will help you to grow spiritually, lead effectively, and finish strong.

Whether you're leading a church, a ministry team, or a small group, this guide will inspire and equip you to serve with focus, humility, and endurance.

Available in Paperback from http://mikeprah.com/bookstore

Also available at Amazon.com, BarnesandNobles.com, Books-a-Million, Walmart.com and several online bookstores and E-book retailers world-wide. For bulk purchases contact: info@mikeprah.com

Skill Will Bring Success: Proven Principles for Living the Life of Your Dreams

Are you putting in the effort but not seeing results? It maybe time to sharpen your edge.

Mike Prah unpacks biblical wisdom and real-life principles to help you develop the emotional, spiritual, and professional skills necessary for lasting success.

With clear teaching, practical tools, and a companion study guide, this book equips you to break through limitations, grow in wisdom, and live the life God intended for you. Skill will bring your success to life.

Available in Hardcover, Paperback, E-Book, and Audio Book at

http://mikeprah.com/bookstore

Also available at Amazon.com and several online bookstores, Audio books, and E-book retailers world-wide including Kindle, Apple Books, Google Books. For bulk purchases contact: info@mikeprah.com.

My Small Group Directory

NAME	PHONE NUMBER	E-MAIL

my notes

my notes

my notes

my notes

CONNECT WITH MIKE PRAH

INSPIRED BY WHAT YOU READ?

Check out the following resources for spiritual guidance and inspiration at www.mikeprah.com.

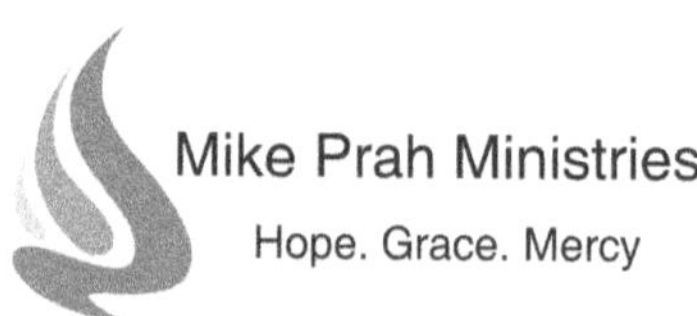

- Online store where you can buy books, merchandise, and special offers at http://mikeprah.com/bookstore

- Book Excerpts and first look at upcoming books

- Video Sermons, Podcasts, Blogs, Journals, and Articles

- Bible Study Lessons

For more information or to book Mike for a speaking engagement, please email info@mikeprah.com

Special Bulk Discounts and Custom Editions:

Most books authored by Mike Prah are available at special discounted rates for bulk purchases by churches, organizations, businesses, and individuals. Customized editions or book excerpts can also be created to meet the specific needs of your ministry, event, or audience. For more information or to inquire about a special order, please email info@mikeprah.com

Signed copies are also available from the author.